ADVENTURES
IN
GOD

A Living Classic Book

ADVENTURES IN GOD

by
John G. Lake

Published by Harrison House, Inc.
P.O. Box 35035
Tulsa, Oklahoma 74153

Harrison House
Tulsa, Oklahoma

Unless otherwise indicated, all Scripture quotations are taken from the *King James Version* of the Bible.

11th Printing
Over 61,000 in Print

Adventures in God
ISBN 0-89274-819-2
Copyright © 1981, 1991 by Harrison House
Formerly ISBN 0-89274-206-2

Published by Harrison House, Inc.
P. O. Box 35035
Tulsa, Oklahoma 74153

Publisher's Preface

We have presented the material in this book as closely as possible to the way in which we received it. There has been no attempt to establish a chronological order. Our hope is that this material will have the same favorable impact on the reader as it had on us when we first read it. Very little editing has been done so that the integrity and flavor of John G. Lake himself would stand.

This manuscript was compiled by John G. Lake's son-in-law, Wilford H. Reidt.

We are deeply grateful to John G. Lake's daughter, Gertrude, and her husband for their careful handling and faithful interest in preserving this valuable manuscript for the benefit of the Body of Christ.

Contents

ADVENTURES
IN
GOD

Foreword

John Graham Lake was a man of prayer and commitment.

To better understand the quality of his life, you will want to read his consecration to God at the close of this book.

At the Lake Healing Rooms in Spokane, Washington, 100,000 healings were recorded in five years. Dr. Ruthlidge of Washington, D.C., called Spokane the healthiest city in the world as a result of Lake's Healing Rooms.

John G. Lake was born March 18, 1870, at St. Mary's, Ontario, Canada. While he was still a child, his parents moved to the United States. At the age of 21, he became a Methodist minister, but later chose to start a newspaper instead of accepting a church ministry.

After his marriage, Lake's wife entered into a prolonged serious illness, but was miraculously delivered under the ministry of John Alexander Dowie in April, 1898. This experience forever altered the direction of John G. Lake's life and ministry.

All that he accomplished as a result of his intense regard for the Word God stands as an example to all Christians of what is possible for any person who will believe and act on the Scriptures.

Chapter 1:

Adventures in God

I found God as a boy, so for years — 50 of them almost — I have been walking in the light of God, understanding fellowship with Him and listening to His Voice.

I want to call to your attention some of the things the Christian enjoys that others miss.

A dear man received an injury that caused his death in a motor accident not far from Beaverton. The day after this man was killed, I was visiting some friends in Beaverton and they told me of his injury. After our visit, my wife and I were driving into the city. As we were coming up one of the highways, a Voice said, "Pull onto the left of the road and stop."

Don't you know that Voice, Christian heart? That Voice is so common that I never even spoke of it to my wife.

The left side is the wrong side of the road, and you are breaking the traffic law to be there. But I have listened to that Voice so many years that I have learned in most cases to obey it. Jesus said, "My sheep know my voice." (John 10:27.)

(The thought I am trying to bring to you, dear friends, is the value of knowing the Lord and what communion with God means. Salvation is not just something God gives you that is going to bless you after you die; it is having the presence of the Lord now. God has promised to the Christian the guidance and direction of the Holy Spirit.)

I pulled onto the left-hand side of the road, ran the wheels of my car close into the ditch, and stopped. Immediately, I heard the grinding of a great truck coming around the curve. I had not seen it before. Instead of coming normally, it was coming down the driver's left-hand side of the road at a 45-degree angle. The truck had gone out of control and was covering the whole road!

If I had been on my side of the road, it would have sideswiped me and pushed me over the bank. A 100-foot drop down! But I was on the other side when the great thing swept past me.

The truck went 50 to 100 feet beyond me, struck a rough spot in the road, and righted itself. The driver got the truck under control and went on.

Dear friends, men in the Word of God were guided by the Voice of God. God talked to them. This is the inner thing of real Christian experience, the reason men seek by the grace of God to enter into the real heart of God — into the real soul of Jesus Christ — into the place where He lives within you — where His Voice speaks in your heart.

I was sitting one day in the home of the DeValeras in Krugersdorp, South Africa, when a man arrived who had traveled all over the country. He had been following me from place to place, trying to catch up with me. He suffered a sunstroke which had affected his mind and he also developed a large cancer.

He came into the house and proved to be a friend of the family.

In a little while a six-year-old child who had been sitting near me went across the room, climbed on the man's knees, put her hands on the cancer on his face, and prayed.

I saw the cancer wither. In half an hour, the thing had disappeared. The wound was still there, but in a few days it was healed.

After the child had laid her hands on top of his head, he arose, saying, "Oh! The fire that has been in my brain has gone out," and his mind was normal.

"Power belongeth unto God" (Ps. 62:11). The simplest soul can touch God and live in the very presence of God and in His power.

It is almost a sadness to my soul that men should be astonished and surprised at an ordinary, tangible evidence of the power of God.

A woman came into the Healing Rooms once with a tumor larger than a full-grown unborn child. Her physicians had been fooled, believing it to be a child until nature's period had passed. Then they decided it must be something else.

She came to the Healing Rooms and I interviewed her. She said, "Mr. Lake, I have the opinion of several physicians. They are all different, but each has said, 'It is possible it may be a child.' But now the time has passed, and they do not know what to say."

I put my hand upon her for a moment, and I said, "Madame, it is not a child; it is a tumor."

She sat down and wept. Her nurse was with her. Her soul was troubled and she did not receive healing.

She came back on another afternoon for prayer and returned the next day wearing her corsets. She said, "I came down to show you that I am perfectly normal. When I retired last night at 10 o'clock, there was no evidence that anything had taken place, beyond that I felt comfortable and the choking was gone. But when I awoke this morning, I was my normal size."

I asked, "Did it disappear in the form of fluid?"

She said, "There was not an outward sign of any character."

Beloved, what happened to it?

It dematerialized. The tumor dissolved.

What is a miracle? It is the tangible evidence of the supreme control of the Spirit of God over every character and form of materiality.

Beloved, the power of such an event, such an act and sign, shows you and me that through living, positive, actual contact with the Spirit of God, all things are possible. Blessed be His name!

I was in a meeting in Los Angeles on one occasion. An old black man was conducting the services.[1] He had the funniest

---

[1] W.J. "Daddy" Seymour, who had attended Charles F. Parham's Bible school in Houston. Although he had not yet received the baptism in the Holy Spirit himself, in the spring of 1906, he felt led to go to California. He received the baptism in the Holy Spirit there and played an important part in the great Azusa Street Revival.

vocabulary. But I want to tell you, there were doctors, lawyers, and professors listening to marvelous things coming from his lips.

It was not what he said in words; it was what he said from his spirit to my heart that showed me he had more of God in his life than any man I had ever met up to that time. It was God in him who was attracting people.

One man insisted on getting up and talking every little while. (Some people have a mania for talking.)

The old black brother endured it for a long time. Finally, the fellow got up again, and the old man stuck his finger out and said, "In the name of Jesus Christ, sit down!"

The man did not sit down — he fell down — and his friends carried him out.

That is only one of the living facts of what Christianity is: the divine power of Jesus Christ by the Holy Spirit, filling a man's soul and body, flashing through his nature like holy flame, accomplishing the will of God.

There is a baptism that belongs to Jesus. It is in His supreme control. No angel or man can bestow it. It comes from Him alone.

He it is "which baptizeth with the Holy Ghost" (John 1:33). So the individual who wants the Holy Spirit must come into definite, conscious contact with Jesus Christ Himself. Bless God! Almost a year before I went to Africa, as I was praying one night, I was overshadowed by the Spirit of the Lord.

The Lord showed me various places in which I would labor for five years and, by the illumination that would appear in the heavens, I knew the extent of the work in each place. The last of these places I saw was South Africa.

That night as I knelt on the floor, I was suddenly present at a church in Johannesburg, South Africa, where an acquaintance of mine was pastor. I walked in the door of the church, walked the entire length of the church to the front and into a little vestry. I looked around the place and took note of everything — the furniture, the room, and all about it. All of this occurred as I prayed in my hometown near Chicago.

In less than a year, I was in that church — and pastor of it. God did the whole thing. I had nothing to do with it.

God having shown with the illumination the marvelous extent and character of the work He was going to do all over the land, I had faith to believe that the thing God showed me would come to pass, and I have lived to see it through.

One evening in my own tabernacle, a young girl about 16 to 18 years of age by the name of Hilda suddenly became overpowered by the Spirit of God.

She arose and stood on the platform beside me. I recognized at once that the Lord had given the girl a message, so I simply stopped preaching and waited while the Spirit of God came upon her.

She began to chant in some language I did not know, then made gestures like those a Mohammedan priest would make when chanting prayers.

In the back of the house I observed a young East Indian, whom I knew. He became enraptured and commenced to walk gradually up the aisle. No one disturbed him, and he proceeded up the aisle until he had reached the front. Then he stood looking into the girl's face with intense amazement.

When her message had ceased, I said to him, "What is it?"

He answered, "Oh, she speaks my language!"

I said, "What does she say?"

He came up on the platform beside me and gave the gist of her message:

"She tells me that salvation comes from God. In order to save men, Jesus Christ, Who was God, became man. She says one man cannot save another; that Mohammed was a man like other men, not a power to save a man from his sins. But Jesus was God, and He had power to impart His Spirit to me and make me like God."

While I was preaching in a church in South Africa, an American lady whose son resided in the state of Iowa, was present in a week night service.

Before the service began, she called me into the vestry and said she had just received a letter from her daughter-in-law. It stated that the woman's son, a college professor, appeared to be tubercular. He was compelled to give up his teaching position and was in a condition of great weakness.

As I conversed with the mother, I observed that she, too, believed her son to be tubercular and that, unless healing came to him quickly, he would die.

I returned to the Audience Room; and as we were about to pray, I stepped to the end of the platform and asked the mother to hand me the letter. Taking it in my hands, I knelt to pray, inviting all present to join me in faith in God for the man's deliverance.

My spirit seemed to ascend in God, and I lost all consciousness of my environment.

Suddenly, I found myself standing in that young man's home in Iowa, nearly 10,000 miles from Johannesburg. The man sat by a hard coal heater with a little boy about two years old on his lap.

I observed him critically and said to myself, *Your face is hard and shows no evidence of soul development or spiritual life, yet your affection for your son is a redeeming quality.*

His wife sat on the opposite side of the table, reading a magazine. Observing her, I remarked to myself, *When he got you, he got a Tartar!*

While standing behind the man's chair, I laid my hands on his head, silently praying for God to impart to him His healing virtue and make the man well — that he might bless the world and that his mother's heart might be comforted.

There was no knowledge of my return. In a moment I was aware that I was kneeling on the church platform. I had been uttering audible prayer and the Spirit of God was resting deeply upon the people.

Some six weeks later, word was received that the young man was quite well. His recovery had begun on the exact date that prayer was offered for him in our church 10,000 miles away.

I was absent from the city of Spokane for a time and, when I returned, Mrs. Lake was not at home. It was just time to leave for my afternoon service when someone came in and said, "Your secretary, Mrs. Graham, is in the throes of death. Your wife is with her."

Immediately I hurried to the place. One of my ministers' wives met me at the door and said, "You are too late; she is gone."

As I stepped inside, the minister was coming out of the room. He said, "She has not breathed for a long time."

But looking on that woman, I thought of how God Almighty had raised her out of death three years before; how He had miraculously given her back her womb, ovaries, and tubes which had been removed in operations; how she had married and conceived a child.

As these thoughts arose, my heart flamed!

I took that woman up off the pillow and called on God for the lightnings of heaven to blast the power of death and deliver her. I commanded her to come back and stay. She came back after having not breathed for 23 minutes!

We have not yet learned to keep in living touch with the powers of God. Once in a while our souls rise, and we see the flame of God accomplish this wonder and that. But, beloved, Jesus Christ lived in the presence of God every hour of the day and night. Never a word proceeded from the mouth of Jesus Christ, but that which was God's Word. He said, "The words that I speak unto you, they are spirit, and they are life" (John 6:63).

When you and I are lost in the Son of God and the fires of Jesus burn in our hearts, as they did in His, our words will be the words of Spirit and of life. There will be no death in them. Beloved, we are on the way.

Having formal acknowledgment as a student of science, it was my privilege to attend clinics, which I frequently did.

At one time I submitted myself to a series of experiments. It was not sufficient to know that God healed; I had to know *how* God healed.

I visited one of the great experimental institutions and submitted myself for a series of experiments.

First, an instrument was attached to my head. This instrument had an indicator that would register the vibrations of the brain.

I began to repeat things like the 23rd Psalm to soothe the mind and reduce its vibrations to the lowest point. Then I repeated the 31st Psalm, the 35th chapter of Isaiah, the 91st Psalm, and Paul's address before Agrippa.

After this, I went into secular literature and recited Tennyson's "Charge of the Light Brigade" and finally Poe's "The Raven" as I prayed in my heart that at the psychological moment, God would anoint my soul in the Holy Spirit.

My difficulty was that while reciting, I could not keep the Spirit from coming upon me. When I finished with "The Raven," those in charge of the experiment said, "You are a phenomenon. You have a wider mental range than any human being we have ever seen."

In reality, this was not so. It was because the Spirit of God kept coming upon me to such degree that I could feel the moving of the Spirit within me.

I prayed in my heart, "Lord God, if You will only let the Spirit of God come like the lightnings of God upon my soul for two seconds, I know something is going to happen that these men have never seen before."

As I recited the last lines of the poem, suddenly the Spirit of God struck me in a burst of praise and tongues. The indicator on that instrument bounded to its limit — and I haven't the least idea how much further it would have gone if it had been possible.

The professors said, "We have never seen anything like it!"

I replied, "Gentlemen, it is the Holy Ghost."

In the second experiment, a powerful X-ray machine with microscopic attachments was connected to my head. The purpose was to see, if possible, what the action of the brain cells was.

I proceeded just as in the former experiment. First, I repeated Scriptures that were soothing — those calculated to reduce the action of the cortex cells to their lowest possible register. Then I went to Scriptures which conveyed better and richer things until I reached the first chapter of John. As I began to recite this, the fires of God began to burn in my heart.

Suddenly, the Spirit of God came upon me as before, and the man who was behind me touched me. It was a signal to me to keep that poise of soul until one after another could look through the instrument.

Finally, when I let go, the Spirit subsided. The professors said, "Why, man, we cannot understand this, but the cortex cells expanded amazingly."

I said to them, "Gentlemen, I want you to see one more thing. Go down in your hospital and bring back a man who has inflammation in the bone. Take your instrument and attach it to his leg. Leave enough space to get my hand on his leg. You can attach it to both sides."

When the instrument was ready, I put my hand on the man's shin and prayed like Mother Etter[2] prays: no strange prayer, but the cry of my heart to God.

I said, "God, kill the devilish disease by Your power. Let the Spirit move in him; let it live in him."

Then I asked, "Gentlemen, what is taking place?"

They replied, "Every cell is responding."

It is so simple: The life of God comes back into the part that is afflicted; immediately the blood flows; the closed, congested cells respond; and the work is done!

That is God's divine science.

Oh, beloved, when you pray, something is happening in you! It is not a myth; it is the action of God.

The Almighty God, by the Spirit, comes into your soul, takes possession of your brain and manifests Himself in the cortex cells of your brain. When you wish and will, either consciously or unconsciously, the *fire* of God — the *power* of God, that *life* of God, that *nature* of God — is transmitted from the cortex cells of your brain and throbs through your nerves down through your person, into every cell of your being — into every cell of your brain, your blood, your flesh, and your bone — into every square inch of your skin, until you are alive with God!

That is divine healing.

---

[2]Maria Woodworth-Etter began preaching in the Midwest in the 1870's and began praying for the sick in 1885 with phenomenal results. She preached into the 1920's. Some consider her to have had the most miraculous ministry in the 20th Century.

One day I sat talking to Father Seymour in Los Angeles. I told him about the following incident in the life of Elias Letwaba, one of our native preachers in South Africa:

I went to his house one day in the country, and his wife said, "He is not home. A little baby is hurt, and he is praying for it."

So I went over to the native hut, got down on my knees, and crawled inside. I saw Letwaba kneeling in a corner by the child. I said, "Letwaba, it is me. What is the matter with the child?"

He told me the mother had been carrying it on her back in a blanket, as natives carry their children, and it fell out. He said, "I think it hurt its neck."

I examined the baby and saw that its neck was broken. It would turn from side to side like the neck of a doll. "Why, Letwaba, the baby's neck is broken!"

I did not have faith for a broken neck, but poor old Letwaba did not know the difference. I saw that he did not understand. He discerned the spirit of doubt in my soul, and I said to myself, *I am not going to interfere with his faith. He will just feel the doubt generated by all the old traditional things I have learned, so I will go outside.*

I went to another hut and kept on praying. I lay down at 1 a.m. At 3 o'clock Letwaba came in.

I said, "Well, Letwaba, how about the baby?"

He looked at me, so lovingly and sweetly, and said, "Why, brother, the baby is all well! Jesus do heal the baby."

I said, "The baby is well! Letwaba, take me to the baby at once."

So we went to the baby. I took the little black thing on my arm and came out of the hut praying: "Lord, take every cursed thing out of my soul that keeps me from believing the Lord Jesus Christ."

As I related the incident to Mr. Seymour, he shouted, "Praise God, brother! That is not healing — it is life!"

In my assembly in Spokane, there was a dear little woman who had been blind for nine years. She had received very little teaching along the line of faith in God.

As she sat at home one day with her six children, she discovered that her dirty brute of a husband had abandoned her and the children, leaving them to starve. (A debased human being is capable of things that no beast will do, for a beast will care for its own.)

You can imagine the effect this had on her little heart. She was crushed, broken, bruised, and bleeding.

They were all sitting together on the front porch of their home. She gathered her children around her and began to pray.

Suddenly one of them got up and said, "Oh, Mama! There is a man coming up the path and he looks like Jesus! And oh, Mama, there is blood on His hands and blood on His feet!"

The children were frightened and ran around the house.

After a while the biggest child looked around the corner and said, "Why, Mama, He is laying His hands on your eyes!"

And just then, her eyes were opened.

That is divine power!

Some years ago there was a farmer in Indiana who used to be a friend of mine. His son, while in South America, had contracted a dreadful case of typhoid fever. Because he had no proper nursing, he developed a great fever sore ten inches in diameter.

His whole abdomen became grown up with proud flesh, one layer on top of another until there were five layers. A nurse had to lift up these layers and wash them with an antiseptic to keep out the maggots.

When he exposed his abdomen to me to pray for him, I was shocked. I had never seen anything like it before. As I began to pray for him, I spread my fingers wide and put my hand right on that cursed growth of proud flesh. I prayed God in the name of Jesus Christ to blast the curse of hell and burn it up by the power of God.

After praying, I took the train back to Chicago. The next day I received a telegram saying, "Lake, the most unusual thing has happened. An hour after you left, the whole print of your hand was burned into that growth a quarter of an inch deep."

You talk about the voltage from Heaven and the power of God! Why there is lightning in the soul of Jesus! The lightnings of Jesus heal men by their flash!

Sin dissolves and disease flees when the power of God approaches!

And yet we are quibbling and wondering if Jesus Christ is big enough to meet our needs.

Take the bars down!

Let God come into your life.

In the name of Jesus, your heart will not be satisfied with an empty Pentecost. But your soul will claim the light of God and the lightnings of Jesus to flood your life!

One day, as a young man, I needed healing from Heaven, but there was nobody to pray for me. I was not even a Christian in the best sense of being a Christian. I was a member of the Methodist church and had seen God heal one dear soul who was very dear to me.

As I sat alone, I said, "Lord, I am finished with the doctor and the devil. I am finished with the world and the flesh. From today forward, I lean on the arm of God."

Right then and there, I committed myself to God; and God Almighty accepted my consecration to Him — although there was no sign of healing.

The disease that almost killed me and had stuck on my life for nearly nine years was gone! It was chronic constipation. I would take three ounces of castor oil at a single dose three times a week.

The place of strength and the place of victory is the place of consecration to God. That victory will come when a man grits his teeth and says, "I go with God this way."

There is no man alive who can define the operations of faith in a man's heart. But one thing we can be sure of: When we cut ourselves off from every other help, we have never found the Lord Jesus Christ to fail. If there are any failures, they are ours, not God's.

Edward Lion was a native man who, until a few years ago, didn't even wear clothes. He was illiterate and knew nothing whatever of our conception of scholarship.

But God anointed that man with the faith of God and a measure of the Holy Ghost so intense that on one occasion when a multitude of sick folk had been brought into a valley, the power of God came upon him and he went upon the mountainside, stretched out his hands over the sick below, and poured out his heart to God.

In a minute, hundreds were healed! Healing power fell upon them.

There is no such instance recorded in the New Testament. Jesus promised that the Last Days would be marked by greater works than He Himself had wrought.

In 1912 I was pastor of the Apostolic Tabernacle, Johannesburg, South Africa.

One of the cardinal teachings of our organization was the ministry of healing through faith in Jesus Christ, the Son of God. The sick were brought from all parts of the land; and thousands were healed through the prayer of faith and the laying on of hands of those who believed.

Our church was then enjoying a great period of spiritual blessing and power. Various remarkable manifestations of the Spirit commonly occurred.

At a Sunday morning service, before public prayer was offered, a member of the congregation arose and requested that those present join in prayer on behalf of his cousin in Wales (7,000 miles across the sea from Johannesburg), that she might be healed. He stated that the woman was violently insane and an inmate of an asylum in Wales.

I knelt on the platform to pray; and an unusual degree of the spirit of prayer came upon my soul, causing me to pray with fervor and power. The spirit of prayer fell upon the audience at the same time.

The people ordinarily sat in their seats and bowed their heads while prayer was being offered, but on this occasion 100 or more in different parts of the house knelt to pray with me. I was uttering the audible prayer; they were praying in silence.

A great consciousness of the presence of God took possession of me. My spirit rose in a great consciousness of spiritual dominion, and I felt for the moment as if I were anointed by the Spirit of God to cast out demons.

My inner, or spiritual, eyes opened. I could see in the spirit and observed that there was a shaft of seeming light, accompanied by moving power, coming from many of those who were praying in the audience.

As the prayer continued, these shafts of light from those who were praying increased in number. Each of them reached my own soul, bringing an increasing impulse of spiritual power — until I seemed well nigh overcome by it.

While this was going on, I was uttering the words of prayer with great force and conscious spiritual power.

Suddenly, I seemed out of the body and, to my surprise, observed that I was rapidly passing over the city of Kimberley, 300 miles from Johannesburg. I was next conscious of the city of Cape Town on the seacoast, a thousand miles away. My next consciousness was of the Island of St. Helena, where Napoleon had been banished; then the Cape Verde lighthouse on the coast of Spain.

By this time it seemed as if I were passing through the atmosphere observing everything, but moving with great lightning-like rapidity.

I remember the passage along the coast of France, across the Bay of Biscay, into the hills of Wales. I had never been in Wales. It was new country to me; and as I passed swiftly over its hills, I said to myself, *These are like the hills of Wyoming along the North Dakota border.*

Suddenly, a village appeared. It was nestled in a deep valley among the hills. Next I saw a public building that I recognized instinctively as the asylum.

On the door I observed an old-fashioned 16th Century knocker. Its workmanship attracted my attention and this thought flashed through my spirit: *That undoubtedly was made by one of the old smiths who manufactured armor.*

I was inside the institution without waiting for the doors to open and present at the side of a cot on which lay a woman. Her wrists and ankles were strapped to the sides of the cot. Another strap had been passed over her legs above the knees, and a second across her breasts. These were to hold her down.

She was wagging her head and muttering incoherently.

I laid my hands upon her head and, with great intensity, commanded in the name of Jesus Christ, the Son of God, that the demon spirit possessing her be cast out and that she be healed by the power of God.

In a moment or two, I observed a change coming over her countenance. It softened and a look of intelligence appeared.

Then her eyes opened, and she smiled up in my face. I knew she was healed.

I had no consciousness whatever of my return to South Africa. Instantly, I was aware that I was still kneeling in prayer, and I was conscious of all the surrounding environment of my church and the service.

Three weeks passed. Then my friend who had presented the prayer request for his cousin came to me with a letter from one of his relatives, stating that an unusual thing had occurred. Their cousin, who had been confined for seven years in the asylum in Wales, had suddenly become well. They had no explanation to offer. The doctors said it was one of those unaccountable things that sometimes occur.

She was perfectly well and had returned home to her friends.

After returning from Africa some years ago, I spent some time visiting my brother and my sister. As we sat together one day, my sister said, "John, I have some neighbors here who are elderly German people and they are having a very hard time.

"First, the old man died; then one of the sisters died. This thing happened, and that thing happened. Finally, the son, who is a shipbuilder, fell and was carried to the hospital. Now gangrene has set in; they say his leg has to be amputated.

"The old mother, a rheumatic cripple, has been sitting in a wheelchair for two and a half years and cannot move."

My brother and I had been having a discussion over this very thing. Jim, a splendid fellow — a professor and well-educated — said, "Jack, don't you think these things are all psychological?"

"Not much," I said.

Jim said, "I think it is. Don't you think healing is a demonstration of the power of mind over matter?"

I said, "No. If that were all it is, you could give just as good a demonstration as I could."

After a while, our sister said, "I have been across the street and have made arrangements for you to go and pray for these people."

I said, "All right. Jim, come along."

When we arrived, I asked the old lady, "Mother, how long have you been in this wheelchair?"

She replied, "Two and a half years. It is awful hard. Not just hard sitting here all the time, but I suffer night and day, with no moment of relaxation from my acute suffering for all this time."

As I listened to her, the flame of God came into my soul. I said, "You rheumatic devil, in the name of Jesus Christ, I will blot you out, if it is the last thing I ever do in the world!" Laying hands on her I looked to Heaven and called on God to cast that devil out and set her free.

Then I said to her, "Mother, in the name of Jesus Christ, get out of your chair and walk!"

And she arose and walked!

My brother said, "My, it beats the devil."

I replied, "That's the intention!"

We went into another room to see the son whose leg was to be amputated. I sat for a few minutes and told him of the power of God. I said, "We have come to you with a message of Jesus Christ, and we have not just come with the message, but with the power of God."

And laying my hands on the limb I said, "In the name of the living God, they shall never amputate this limb!"

The leg was healed.

After about six months, I again stopped at my sister's home. The young lady from across the street called and said, "You must come across and see my mother and brother. They are so well."

When I called, I found the old lady was very happy. I asked about her son. She said, "Oh, Jake, he is not at home. Why, he is so well that he went down to the saloon and danced all night!"

I waited to see Jake and tried to tell him something about the living God that he had felt in his body and Who wanted to take possession of his soul and reveal the nature of Jesus Christ in him.

Five years passed. When I again stopped at my sister's home, she said, "Do you remember the people you prayed for across the road? Here is Jake now, coming from work."

We sat on the porch and talked. I said, "Well, Jake, how is it?"

"Oh," he said, "I do not understand it all, but something has been going on. It is in me. First, I could not go to the dance. Next, I could not drink beer; then my tobacco did not taste good; and then a joy came into my heart. I found it was Jesus."

This man had been *born of God* — his nature brought into union with God by the Holy Spirit. Blessed be His precious Name!

A few days after my arrival in Johannesburg, the superintendent of one of the great missionary societies said, "Our native pastor, who has the church a few doors from your home, must leave for six weeks. Will you occupy the pulpit of the native church until you are ready to undertake your own work?"

This was God's first door. I instantly accepted!

On Sunday afternoon I preached to a congregation of 500 Zulus through a proficient interpreter, a woman missionary who had lived among the Zulus for 30 years.

As the meeting progressed, a spiritual condition developed almost similar to the dreaded silence — the deep stillness — that permeates the atmosphere preceding a cyclone.

This condition in the Spirit climaxed suddenly as, by a single impulse, the native audience burst into prayer. Everyone prayed — saints and sinners alike — but no one came to the altar. No invitation was given.

God had come in overwhelming conviction for sin, and we were impressed that it was not the mind of God to begin to reap until God Himself thrust in the sickle.

I feel, out of life's experience as a Holy Ghost preacher, that great damage is done by not waiting for a real ripeness of the work of the Holy Spirit in the soul of an audience. So frequently, an invitation is given and pressure is put on the audience to bring souls to the altar before God's ripeness of conviction unto repentance is complete.

At the close of the meeting my interpreter said, "In all my missionary experience, I have never before seen such a spirit of prayer on a native audience."

The next meeting took place at 7 o'clock that evening. A quiet stillness pervaded the meeting — God was searching hearts.

I preached on repentance: real repentance, hundredfold repentance, Holy Ghost repentance, heaven's *metanoia* — the completeness of separation from the world, its sin and its spirit, like Jesus separated Himself unto all righteousness at the River Jordan. (Matt. 3:13-15.)

Suddenly, a man arose in the back of the audience and started for the altar. When he was about ten feet away from the altar, the Spirit of the Lord struck him and he fell flat on his face.

Another man arose and walked calmly and steadily to the front. When he came to where the first man had fallen, the Spirit of the Lord struck him and he fell on top of No. 1!

One after another, they began to come forward. Each one in turn fell at the same spot until fifteen men were piled, one on top of another.

It was a hot, sultry night. I was troubled because on the very bottom of the pile was a little man lying on his face. The next man lay on top of him, pressing the first man's face into the floor, and I was afraid he would smother.

I had never witnessed such a situation before. I had seen many wonderful manifestations of God, but none like this.

Soon my human sympathy for the little fellow on the bottom of the pile overcame me. I stooped down and tried to pull two or three of these men off him; but they were so piled up, one on top of another, that it seemed impossible to reach him.

The Spirit of the Lord spoke within my soul and said, "If God has slain these, can you not trust Him to keep them from smothering?"

I replied, "Excuse me, Lord," and returned to my seat on the platform.

My interpreter was greatly disturbed. She said, "Dr. Lake, what will you do now?"

I replied, "The Lord is doing this. We will just wait and see what the Holy Ghost does and learn how He does it. Remember, sister, He made known his ways unto Moses, his acts unto the children of Israel (Ps. 103:7). We have seen His acts — strange ones. Perhaps we can now learn His ways."

We sat quietly. In about fifteen minutes one of the prostrate men began to confess his sin at the top of his voice. It was a wholehearted soul confession of such evident thoroughness! After a short time, he arose with the light of God in his face and returned to his seat.

By that time another man was confessing, and then another and another, until the whole fifteen men had poured out their souls to God and returned to their seats.

I indicated to the interpreter that I wanted the first man brought to me (the little fellow for whom I had been distressed) so I could question him.

He was a Zulu native who worked for a Dutch family. They had given him a Dutch name, Willum.

I said, "Willum, tell me: What took place while you lay on the floor?"

He said to me in Dutch, "Oh, boss, (This was the manner in which the native always addressed a white man) while I lay on the floor, Jesus come to me, and Jesus say, 'Willum, I take all your sins away.' And Jesus go away. Then Jesus come again. And Jesus put His hand upon my heart, moved it up and down, and say, 'Willum, I make your heart all white.' "

Willum looked into my face. He was all glorified with the light of Heaven until his face was like the face of an angel. He said, "My heart all white! My heart all white!"

He and his friend remained in the church and sang all night. At 6 o'clock the next morning, they both went to their work.

On Wednesday night, my wife and I sat on the platform together. Willum and his friend came early and sat on the front seat.

Mrs. Lake asked, "John, who is the boy sitting on the front seat?"

I replied, "This is the boy with whom I was so impressed Sunday night."

"John, Jesus told me just now if I would lay my hands on that boy, He would baptize him with the Holy Ghost."

"Then go to him at once."

She laid her hands on him. In three minutes he was filled with the Holy Ghost, speaking in tongues, glorifying God, and prophesying.

Close to a South African city in which I was ministering, there were hills with outcroppings of rocks — like a series of cliffs, one above another. I would go up into these hills to be alone and rest.

One day I observed a lady bringing a young child and setting him on one of the shelves above a small cliff. She left the child some food and water. It seemed a dangerous thing to do, since the child might fall and hurt himself. However, I observed that the child was crippled and could not move around.

After his mother left, I went over to him, laid my hands on him, and prayed. Immediately the child bounded off down the hill to catch his mother.

Not caring to meet anyone, I moved around the hill out of sight.

One day a woman came to the Healing Rooms in the old Rookery Building in Spokane. She could not raise her arm. She said she had an open sore on her side and could get no help from physicians. She added that she had no faith — in doctors, in man, in God, or in Jesus Christ — but asked if I could help her.

I prayed for her three times with no results. After the third time I said to God, "God, her soul is closed. Open her soul that she might receive."

The next morning as she was putting up her hair, she suddenly discovered that she was using the bad arm and had it raised up to her head. She felt her side, and the open sore was gone.

Immediately, she telephoned to tell us about it.

I said, "Sister, come down here. There are people waiting to hear your testimony."

How much faith does God require of the person who comes and asks?

A closing sentence of an interpretation of tongues given in June, 1910, in Somerset, East Cape Colony, South Africa:

"Christ is at once the spotless descent of God into man, and the sinless ascent of man into God, and the Holy Spirit is the Agent by whom this is accomplished."

A *holy mind* cannot repeat a vile thing, nor be the creator of a vile suggestion. It is an unholy mind that is capable of such an act. I say with Paul, "Mark such a person" (Rom. 16:17). He may talk, but he does not know God. He does not comprehend the power of salvation, nor is he the possessor of the Holy Spirit.

Chapter 2:

How the Lord Sent Me to South Africa

I planned to go to Africa as a boy. I looked forward to it through my young manhood.

Shortly after my baptism in the Holy Spirit, a working of the Spirit commenced in me that seemed to have for its purpose the revelation of the nature of Jesus Christ to me and in me.

Through this guardianship and remolding of the Spirit, a great tenderness for mankind was awakened in my soul. I saw mankind through new eyes. They seemed to me as wandering in the midst of confusion, having strayed far, groping and wandering hither and thither. They had no definite aim and did not seem to understand what the difficulty was, or how to return to God.

The desire to proclaim the message of Christ and to demonstrate His power to save and bless grew in my soul, until my life was swayed by this overwhelming passion.

However, my heart was divided. I could not follow successfully the ordinary pursuits of life and business. When a man came into my office, though I knew that twenty or thirty minutes of concentration on the business at hand would possibly net me thousands of dollars, I could not discuss business with him.

By a new power of discernment I could see his soul and understand his inner life and motives. I recognized him as one of these wandering sheep and longed with an overwhelming desire to help him find God and find himself.

This division in my soul between business interests and the desire to help men find God became intense. In many instances what should have been a successful business interview and the closing of a great business transaction ended in a prayer meeting. I would invite the individual to kneel with me while I poured out my heart to God on his behalf.

I determined to discuss the matter with the president of my company and frankly told him the condition of soul I found myself in and its cause.

He kindly replied: "You have worked hard, Lake. You need a change. Take a vacation for three months. If you want to preach, preach. But at the end of the three months, $50,000 a year will look like a lot of money to you, and you will have little desire to sacrifice it for dreams of religious possibilities."

I thanked him, accepted an invitation to join a brother in evangelistic work, and left the office, never to return.

During those three months I preached every day to large congregations, saw a multitude of people saved from their sins and healed of their diseases, and hundreds of them baptized in the Holy Ghost. At the end of the three months, I said to God: "I am through forever with everything in life but the proclamation and demonstration of the Gospel of Jesus Christ."

I disposed of my estate, distributed my funds in a manner I believed to be for the best interests of the Kingdom of God, made myself wholly dependent upon God for the support of myself and family, and abandoned myself to the preaching of Jesus.

While ministering in a city in northern Illinois, the chore boy at the hotel where we were staying asked for help in sawing down a large tree. I volunteered to assist him. As we sawed the tree, the Spirit of the Lord spoke within my spirit clearly and distinctly: "Go to Indianapolis. Prepare for a winter campaign. Get a large hall. In the spring you will go to Africa."

(It all came to pass. It is power. Power is manifest in many ways. There is a power of *faith* which draws to you what seems impossible.)

I returned to the hotel and told my wife of the incident. She said: "I knew several days ago that your work here was done, for as I prayed the Spirit said to me, 'Your husband is going on.'"

I went to Indianapolis and the Lord directed in a marvelous way. In a few days I had secured a large hall and began conducting services, as He had directed.

One day during the following February (after I had been preaching some time), my preaching partner said to me, "John, how much will it cost to take our party to Johannesburg, South Africa?"

I replied, "Two thousand dollars."

"Well, if we are going to Africa in the spring, it is time that you and I were praying for the money."

"Tom, I have been praying for the money ever since New Year's. I have not heard from the Lord or from anyone else concerning it."

"Never mind. Let's pray again."

We went to Tom's room and knelt down by his bed in prayer.

After some time he slapped me on the back, saying, "Don't pray anymore, John. Jesus told me just now that He would send us that two thousand dollars, and it would be here in four days."

Four days later Tom returned from the post office and threw out upon the table four $500 drafts, saying, "John, there is the answer. Jesus has sent it. We are going to Africa."

The gift of money had been sent to Tom by a friend with a letter. The letter read, "I was standing in the bank at Monrovia, California, and something said to me, "Send Tom Hezmalhaltz two thousand dollars.' It is yours, Tom, for whatever purpose God has shown you."

I never knew who wrote the letter, as he desired that no one else know.

We went straight out and purchased the tickets for the entire party to travel from Indianapolis, Indiana, to Johannesburg, South Africa. There were twelve of us — my family of eight and four others.

We had our tickets to Africa, but there would be many other expenses en route. I had only $1.50 in hand.

As our train pulled out of the station at Indianapolis, a young man who had worked as my secretary ran alongside the train and threw a two-dollar bill through the window. That gave us a total of $3.50.

A young lady, who had been one of our workers, was traveling with us as far as Detroit, Michigan. I needed $10 to buy her a ticket to northern Michigan.

As we rode along, I said to my wife, "Jen, when we reach Detroit, I will need $10 for Winnie's railway ticket; but I have no money." So we bowed our heads and prayed.

We always followed this practice concerning our needs. We never told anyone what our needs were, but we always told the Lord.

When we arrived in Detroit, my brother and married sister were there to meet us and with them was my younger brother, Jim.

As I stepped off the train, Jim took me by the arm and walked across the station with me. Then he said, "Jack, I hope you won't be mad, but I would like to give you this," and he pulled out of his wallet a ten-dollar bill and slipped it into my vest pocket.

I thanked him, turned about, and went to purchase Winnie's ticket.

I still had $3.50. We purchased some canned beans and other edibles which we used on the train en route to St. Johns, New Brunswick.

When we finally arrived at the ship for Liverpool, I had $1.25 left. On board I gave 50¢ to the table steward and 50¢ to the bedroom steward. When we reached England, I still had 25¢.

We remained five days in Liverpool at the expense of the transportation company, waiting for the second ship.

One day Mrs. Lake said to me, "What about our laundry?"

I replied, "Send it down. I have no money, but perhaps the Lord will meet us before we need to get it." Being very busy, I forgot about it entirely.

On the last night of our stay in Liverpool, just after I had retired about midnight, my wife said, "How about the laundry?"

I replied, "I'm sorry, but I forgot it."

"Just like a man! Now I'll tell you about it. I knew you didn't have any money, neither did I. So I prayed about it. After praying, I felt that I should go down to the laundry and inquire what the amount of the bill was. It was $1.65. As I was returning to the hotel, I passed a gentleman on the street. He said, 'Pardon me, but I feel I should give you this.' He handed me a number of coins. I returned to the laundry, counted it out to the laundryman, and found it was just the amount of the bill."

We rejoiced in this little evidence of God's presence with us.

The next morning we left by train for London and that evening boarded our ship for South Africa.

At that time, I had an English shilling. When our ship stopped at Madeira, one of the Canary Islands, I purchased a shilling's worth of fruit for the children — and the last penny was gone.

Through my knowledge of the immigration laws of South Africa, I knew that before we would be permitted to land, I must show the immigration inspector that I possessed at least $125. We prayed earnestly over this matter. About the time we reached the Equator, a rest came into my soul concerning it, and I could pray no more.

About eight or ten days later we arrived in Cape Town harbor, and our ship anchored. The immigration inspector came on board and the passengers lined up at the purser's office to present their money and receive their tickets to land.

My wife said, "What are you going to do?"

"I am going to line up with the rest. We have obeyed God this far. It is now up to the Lord."

As I stood in line, awaiting my chance to explain our dilemma, a fellow passenger suddenly tapped me upon the shoulder and indicated that I should step out of the line and walk over to the ship's rail to speak with him. He asked me some questions, then he drew from his pocket a traveller's checkbook. He handed me two money orders totalling 42 pounds sterling, or $200.

He said, "I feel led to give this to help your work."

Johannesburg is 1,000 miles inland from Cape Town. Throughout the voyage we earnestly prayed about the subject of a home. As faith missionaries, we had neither a Board nor friends behind us to furnish money. We were dependent upon God. Many times during the trip to Johannesburg, we bowed our heads and reminded God that when we arrived there we would need a home.

Upon our arrival, as we stepped ashore, I observed a little woman bustling up, whom I instantly recognized to be an American.

She stepped up to Tom and said, "You are an American missionary party?"

He replied, "Yes."

"How many are there in your party?"

"Four."

"No," she said, "You are not the family. Is there any other?"

He said, "Yes. Mr. Lake."

Turning to me, she said, "How many are in your family?"

I answered, "My wife, myself, and seven children only."

"Oh," she said, "You are the family."

"What is it, madam?"

"While in prayer last night, God told me to meet this boat, and there would be upon it an American missionary with a family of nine, consisting of two adults and seven children, and that I was to give them a home."

At 3 o'clock that same afternoon, we were in a furnished cottage in Johannesburg. God had provided the home for us.

Our beloved benefactor was an American missionary, Mrs. C. L. Goodenough. She remained our beloved friend and fellow worker in the Lord.

And that is how we got to Africa.

Chapter 3:

How I Came To Devote My Life to the Ministry of Healing

*N*o one can understand the tremendous hold the revelation of Jesus as a present-day Healer took on my life, and what it meant to me, unless they first understand my environment.

I was one of 16 children. Our parents were strong, vigorous, healthy people. My mother died at the age of 75, and my father, still lives at the time of this writing[1] and is 77.

Before my knowledge and experience of the Lord as our Healer, we buried eight members of the family. A strange train of sicknesses, resulting in death, had followed the family. For 32 years some member of our family was an invalid. During this long period, our home was never without the shadow of sickness.

---

[1]March, 1918

As I think back over my boyhood and young manhood, there comes to mind remembrances like a nightmare: sickness, doctors, nurses, hospitals, hearses, funerals, graveyards, and tombstones; a sorrowing household; a brokenhearted mother and grief-stricken father, struggling to forget the sorrows of the past, in order to assist the living members of the family who needed their love and care.

When Christ was revealed to us as our Healer, my brother — who had been an invalid for 22 years, upon whom Father had spent a fortune for unavailing medical assistance — was dying. He bled incessantly from his kidneys and was kept alive through the assimilation of blood-creating foods which produced blood almost as fast as it flowed from his person. I have never known any man to suffer so extremely and for so long as he did.

A sister, 34 years of age, was then dying with five cancers in her left breast. Before being turned away to die, she had been operated on five times at a large hospital in Detroit, Michigan, by a German surgeon of repute. After the operations, four other "heads" developed, making five cancers in all.

Another sister lay dying of an issue of blood. Day by day, her life blood flowed away until she was in the very throes of death.

In my own life and circumstances, there were similar conditions. I had married and established my own home; but very soon after marriage, the same train of conditions that had followed my father's family seemed to appear in mine. My wife became an invalid from heart disease and tuberculosis. She would lose her heart action and lapse into unconsciousness. Sometimes I would find her lying unconscious on the floor or in her bed, having been suddenly stricken.

Stronger and stronger stimulants became necessary to revive her heart until we were using nitroglycerine tablets in a final, heroic effort to stimulate the action of her heart.

After these heart spells, she would remain in a semi-paralytic state for weeks, (the result of over stimulation, the physicians said).

But suddenly, in the midst of the deepest darkness, when baffled physicians stood back and acknowledged their inability to help, when the cloud of darkness and death was again hovering over the family — the message of one godly minister, great enough and true enough to God to proclaim the whole truth of God, brought the light of God to our souls!

We took our dying brother to a Healing Home in Chicago, where prayer was offered for him with the laying on of hands. He received an instant healing and arose from his deathbed a well man. He walked four miles, returned home, and took a partnership in our father's business.

Great joy and a marvelous hope sprang up in our hearts! A real manifestation of the healing power of God was before us. We quickly arranged to take our sister who suffered from cancers, to the same Healing Home. We had to take her there on a stretcher. As we carried her into the healing meeting, she was speaking within her soul, *Others may be healed because they are so good, but I fear healing is not for me.* It seemed more than her soul could grasp.

But after listening from her cot to the preaching and teaching of the Word of God on healing through Jesus Christ, hope sprang up in her soul. She was prayed for and hands were laid on her. As the prayer of faith arose to God, the power of God descended upon her, thrilling her being. Her pain instantly vanished! The swelling disappeared gradually. The large core cancer turned black and in a few days fell out. The smaller ones disappeared. The mutilated breast began to re-grow, and it became a perfect breast again.

How our hearts thrilled! Words alone cannot tell this story! A new faith sprang up within us. If God could heal our dying brother and our dying sister, causing cancers to disappear, He could heal anything or anybody!

Then our sister with the issue of blood began to look to God for her healing. She and her husband were devout Christians, and although they prayed, their prayers seemed unanswered for a time. Then one night I received a telephone call and was told that if I wished to see her in this life, I must come to her bedside at once.

Upon arriving, I found that death was already upon her. She had passed in unconsciousness. Her body was cold. No pulse was discernable. Our parents knelt, weeping beside her bed, and her husband knelt at the foot of the bed, in sorrow. Her baby lay in his crib.

A great cry to God, such as had never before come from my soul, went up to God. She must not die! I would not have it! Had not Christ died for her? Had not God's healing power been manifested for the others, and should she not likewise be healed?

No words of mine can convey to another soul the cry that was in my heart and the flame of hatred for death and sickness that the Spirit of God had stirred within me. The very wrath of God seemed to possess my soul!

After telephoning and telegraphing some believing friends for assistance in prayer, we called on God. I rebuked the power of death in the name of Jesus Christ. In less than an hour, we rejoiced to see the evidence of returning life. My sister was thoroughly healed! Five days later she came to my father's home and joined the family for Christmas dinner.

My wife, who had been slowly dying for years, suffering untold agonies, was the last of the four to receive God's healing touch. But, oh, before God's power came upon her, I realized as never before the character of consecration God was asking and what a Christian should give to God.

Day by day, death silently stole over her. Then the final hours came. A brother minister who was present walked over and stood at her bedside. Then returning to me with tears in his eyes, he said, "Be reconciled to let your wife die."

I thought of my babies. I thought of her whom I loved as my own soul, and a flame burned in my heart. I felt as if God had been insulted by such a suggestion! Yet I had many things to learn.

In the midst of my soul-storm, I returned home, picked up my Bible from the mantelpiece, and threw it on the table. If ever God caused a man's Bible to open to a message his soul needed, surely He did it then for me.

The Book opened at the 10th chapter of Acts, and my eyes fell on the 38th verse, which read, "God anointed Jesus of

Nazareth with the Holy Ghost and with power: who went about doing good, and healing all that were oppressed of the *devil*; for God was with him."

Like a flash from the blue, these words pierced my heart: *Oppressed of the devil!* So, God was not the author of sickness! And the people whom Jesus healed had not been made sick by God!

Hastily taking a reference to another portion of the Word, I read the words of Jesus in Luke 13:16: "Ought not this woman . . . whom *Satan hath bound,* lo, these eighteen years, be loosed from this bond?" Once again Jesus attributed sickness to the devil.

What a faith sprang up in my heart! What a flame of knowledge concerning the Word of God and the ministry of Jesus went over my soul! I saw as never before why Jesus healed the sick: He was doing the will of His Father; and in doing His Father's will, He was destroying the works of the devil. (Heb. 2:14.)

I said in my soul, *This work of the devil — this destruction of my wife's life — in the name of Jesus Christ shall cease, for Christ died and Himself took our infirmities and bare our sicknesses.*

We decided on 9:30 a.m. as the time when prayer would be offered for my wife's recovery. Again, I telephoned and telegraphed friends to join me in prayer.

At 9:30 I knelt at her deathbed and called on the living God. The power of God came upon her, thrilling her from head to feet. Her paralysis left, her heart became normal, her cough ceased, her breathing became regular, and her temperature became normal. The power of God was flowing through her, seemingly as blood flows through veins.

As I prayed, I heard a sound from her lips — not the sound of weakness as before, but a strong, clear voice. She cried out, "Praise God, I am healed!" With that, she caught hold of the bed clothing, threw it back, and in a moment was standing on the floor.

What a day! Will I ever forget it? The power of God thrilled our souls, and the joy of God possessed our hearts because of her recovery.

The news spread throughout the city, the state, and the nation. Newspapers discussed it and our home became a center of inquiry. People traveled great distances to see and talk with her. She was flooded with letters.

A new light dawned in our souls. The church had diligently taught us that the days of miracles had passed, and believing this, eight members of the family had been permitted to die. But, now, with the light of truth flashing in our hearts, we saw that as a lie, no doubt invented by the devil and diligently heralded as truth by the church, thus robbing mankind of its rightful inheritance through the blood of Jesus.

People came to our home, saying, "Since God has healed you, surely He will heal us. Pray for us." We were forced into it. God answered, and many were healed.

Many years have passed since then, but no day has gone by in which God has not answered prayer. I have devoted my life, day and night, to this ministry, and people have been healed — not by ones and twos, nor by hundreds, or even by thousands, but by tens of thousands.

In due time, God called me to South Africa, where I witnessed a manifestation of the healing power of God such as the world perhaps has not seen since the days of the apostles.

Christian men were baptized in the Holy Ghost, went forth in the mighty power of God, proclaiming the name of Jesus and laying hands on the sick. And the sick were healed! Sinners, witnessing these evidences of the power of God, cried out in gladness and gave themselves to the service of God.

Like it was in the days of Jesus: "There was great joy in that city" — and that nation. (Acts 8:8.)

Finally, God brought me to Spokane, where we have ministered to hundreds of sick persons each week. The city is filled with the praises of God because of the blessed manifestations of God's healing power everywhere. People have come from as far as 5,000 miles away for healing. Some have written letters. Others have telegraphed. Some have cabled from halfway 'round the world, asking for prayer, and God has graciously answered.

Ministers and churches throughout the land have seen that, although the church has taught that the days of miracles only belonged to the times of the apostles, that statement was a falsehood. They have seen that the healing power of God is as available to the honest soul today as it was in the days of Christ on the earth. "The gifts and callings of God are without repentance," and Jesus is the Healer still.

Chapter 4:

More Adventures in God

*D*uring my ministry in South Africa, I came across a bachelor who hated everything that was Christian. He had a reputation for cussing preachers off his place.

One day I realized that he had not been seen for a while, so I decided to pay him a visit. Immediately, I was warned as to what kind of a reception I could expect. I went anyway.

Upon entering his home, I observed that he was a very sick man. Before he could say a thing, I tossed my hat down, prayed that God would heal him, and left.

A few days later he came to church. He was a changed man!

The Christian, the child of God, the Christ-man who has committed his body as well as his spirit and soul to God, ought not be a subject for healing. He ought to be a subject of continuous, abiding health, because he is filled with the life of God.

Jesus Christ is at once the *law* and *life* of God.

When I lived in Africa, one of our departments was the native work. I bless God for the marvels He let me witness among the native people. I believe we had a privilege never accorded any other white man in modern times.

In Basutoland, on Christmas Eve, 1912, the Lord's Supper was administered to 75 healed lepers. They had been healed under the ministry of a black fellow whose sole raiment when we first knew him was a goatskin apron.

It was a beautiful thing to sit with a man under whose ministry 75 lepers had been healed! Some were without noses; others without fingers, or toes, or ears.

But I am going to tell you another leper story. Until about seven weeks ago, a man by the name of Young was quarantined in the State of Nebraska. Correspondence with him was made possible through a senator, another leper.

Reared as a Roman Catholic, Young believed in the power of faith. God told him He was going to move in behalf of this deliverance.

Officers of the institution discovered that he had been sending and receiving letters, contrary to instructions.

When confronted, Young said, "Yes, I have been corresponding with people who pray the prayer of faith that I shall not die like a dog or pig."

The officers asked to see the letters. In a few days they came back to him and said, "If you think you can get healed, we will turn you loose on your pledge that you will go directly to Spokane to these people who heal."

So he started for Spokane with their pledge to furnish him with the necessary funds.

The day before I left Spokane, I sat down with that man and he dictated the story of his healing by the power of God. He joined his wife and children in Key West.

My Lord is not dead! But I'll tell you, dear hearts — we have been satisfied to live in Christ in our babyhood, to perpetuate our babyhood, and to go on shouting like a lot of babies, instead of entering into the secrets of the heart of Jesus Christ by the grace of God and claiming from Heaven the divine flames of God upon our souls.

When that takes place, then we shall stand amazed at the action of God in our own and others' lives.

A Mrs. McDonald was brought to the Healing Rooms so emaciated by tuberculosis that she weighed only 70 pounds. Her condition improved so rapidly that she put on flesh at the rate of one pound per day.

She attended our Divine Healing Meeting and gave public testimony to her healing.

An hour later she called us on the telephone, exclaiming, "I am so happy I just had to tell somebody. I have walked all the way home, kindled the fire in two stoves, and am preparing supper — a thing I have not been able to do for over a year."

A 12-year-old boy suffering from tuberculosis of the spine, so extreme that he was compelled to wear a steel jacket both day and night, was brought to the Healing Rooms a few days for prayer.

In less than ten days, his condition was so improved that he discarded the jacket entirely. His shoulders had straightened; the vertebrae remained fixed, and the boy returned to his home at Rosalia, praising God that He had proven in our own city in March, 1919, that Jesus Christ is still the Healer.

At Cookhouse, Cape Colony, there were ten brothers by the name of Watson — men who had been saved and baptized in the Holy Ghost.

As I was conducting a meeting at the home of one of them, the Spirit fell upon the youngest of the family. He arose and we observed that he was giving the arrangements for a drama. He was perfectly under the power of the Spirit. He had no consciousness in the natural of what was taking place.

All at once, the Spirit fell upon another of the brothers, then another and another until all ten became actors in the same drama.

We sat there amazed for hours, observing a perfect five-act drama — a presentation of God's dealings with the race of man throughout the history of the world.

I left that night with the awe of God on my soul so deep that, for weeks afterwards, I felt as if I wanted to walk very softly.

The life of the Christian without the indwelling power of the Spirit in the heart is a weariness to the flesh. It is an obedience to commandments and an endeavor to walk according to a pattern which you have not power to follow.

But, bless God, the Christian life that is lived by the impulse of the Spirit of Christ within your soul becomes a joy, a power, and a glory.

Easter, 1916

When preaching at Bloemfontein, Orange Free State, a man by the name of Johnson, an epileptic for twelve years, attended the meetings. He had been suffering 12 to 15 seizures a day.

After the service, a group of us were in an attitude of prayer and communion with God preparatory to going out for an open-air meeting.

Someone turned and asked this young man if he would like to be a Christian.

He said, "Well, I guess not. I would do the same things tomorrow I have done today if I were."

Like a flash out of the blue, the Spirit of God fell upon him and he fell prostrate upon the floor, remaining there until 10 o'clock the next morning.

Before morning, that fellow who had been having about 15 seizures a day was not only saved, but healed. He went forth at 10 o'clock, baptized in the Holy Ghost.

One day our minister at Bloemfontein was going out to conduct a meeting for Basuto natives. He could not speak enough Basuto to preach to them, so it was necessary for him to have an interpreter. Johnson was with him.

The interpreter did not arrive. But when time came for the meeting to begin, the power of God came upon Johnson. To the amazement of all, he stood and spoke forth the Word to those native people in the purest Basuto!

One evening as I was preaching, the Spirit of the Lord descended upon a man in the front row, a minister from London, England.

He remained in a sitting posture, but began rising from the chair. Gradually, he came down the chair; then gradually, he began to rise again, somewhat higher. This was repeated three times.

Was it a reversal of the law of gravitation?

I think not.

My own conception is that his soul became so united with the Spirit of God that the attractive power of God was so intense it drew him up.

One day I stood at the railway station in Logansport, Indiana, waiting for my train and observing a group of Italian men, apparently laborers, sitting on a bench. They were going somewhere to work.

As I walked up and down the platform, I said, "Oh, God, how much I would like to be able to talk to these men about the Living Christ and His power to save!"

The Spirit said, "You can."

I stepped over to them; and as I preached, I observed myself beginning to speak in some foreign language.

I addressed one of the group, and he instantly answered me in Italian. I asked where he was from, and he replied, "Naples."

For fifteen minutes God let me tell the truths of Christ and the power of God to that group of laborers in Italian, a language of which I had no knowledge.

That was a little flash — a gleam — but one day, bless God, there will come from Heaven a shower that will so anoint the souls of men that they will speak in every language man speaks by the power of God. "And this gospel of the kingdom shall be preached in all the world for a witness unto all nations; and then shall the end come" (Matt. 24:14).

While I was in Africa, the Church of England sent a three-man delegation to Johannesburg for a year to report back to England concerning our work in South Africa.

The result was a great conference of Church of England preachers was called and I was asked to preach at the conference.

It resulted in the establishment of healing societies in the Church of England.

We were blessed recently in this country with one of their "healers," Mr. Hicks, who held meetings in the various Episcopal churches all around the land.

I have just come from Portland, where the streets were filled for ten blocks around the church with automobiles carrying the sick to his meetings.

Mr. Clark Mitchell was in a logging accident ten years ago in which his left side was severely injured — the knee and left shoulder were crushed.

For ten years he experienced great suffering. His knee developed a tumor so large that it filled his pant leg.

He told me there were occasions when he was able to walk perhaps a single block, but with great suffering. Other periods he was compelled to be confined to his home and his chair.

One day as I was hurrying down Pacific Avenue on the way to my meeting at the Free Methodist Church, I passed Mr. Mitchell's home and his daughter waved to me.

She had seen me coming and said to her father, "I see Mr. Lake, and I am going to call him in."

Mr. Mitchell replied, "No, don't do it. I don't take any stock in that kind of stuff."

Though I knew nothing of these circumstances, I would have paid no attention if I had. I am Scotch.

When I entered their home, I said, "Mr. Mitchell, I have no time to talk to you."

I threw off my overcoat and hat, and knelt to pray. He indicated it was his knee, so I laid my hands on his knee and began to pray. As I did, I was conscious that he was healed.

I said, "Mr. Mitchell, stick out your leg." He did.

"Get up and walk." He did.

As he walked, he kept saying "I don't understand. I don't understand." He came back and sat down, still saying, "I don't understand."

"What is it you do not understand, brother?"

"Why, I cannot understand God's healing me. I am not a Christian."

I said, "Is it possible you have not yet given your heart to God?"

He said "It is."

"Then, brother, in the name of the Lord, let us do it now."

So he, his dear daughter, and another lady, knelt with me and all three yielded their hearts to the Lord Jesus Christ.

As he sat in his chair, I told him of the healing of another man and how the bones would grind in his hip.

Mr. Mitchell said, "That is like my shoulder."

This is when I first learned he had a bad shoulder, so I called his daughter again, and we prayed for his shoulder.

Then I said, "Put up your arm, brother."

When he raised his arm, I asked him if it was perfectly free.

He replied, "Perfectly free."

By 8:30 p.m. the tumor that had been on his knee for ten years had totally disappeared.

The next morning, he went to the printing office, presented himself to the editor, and said, "Mr. Scott, I am the man the Lord has healed." And the newspaper editor wrote up a statement about the man's healing.

The same day he spaded his entire garden.

The day after, he went to work for a plasterer where he continued work.

The day of miracles had not passed as of this incident. March, 1922, in Forest Grove, Oregon.

Dominion

Now I want to teach you something of the inner things of healing that people are not aware of.

There is a conscious dominion Jesus Christ gives to the Christian soul. It was that thing in the soul of Peter when he met the lame man at the Beautiful Gate.

Instead of praying for the man's healing, Peter said, "In the name of Jesus Christ of Nazareth rise up and walk" (Acts 3:6). No prayer about it; no intercession.

Peter exercised the dominion that was in his soul. The divine flash of the power of God went forth from his soul, and the man instantly arose and went with them into the Temple "walking and leaping, and praising God" (v.8).

Sometimes those who minister to the sick are aware of what takes place, although the individual himself is unaware of any healing. There is a dominion in the soul of the real man of God who is in touch with Heaven. When the real thing takes place — when a person is saved or healed from disease — we know what it is. We pray until we are satisfied in our souls that the work is complete.

In the same building that we had our Healing Rooms, there was an X-ray laboratory. The technicians wanted to see what it was all about, so they asked to take X-rays at no charge to us of some of our prospects for healing. It was a unique opportunity.

Among those we sent to them was a man with tuberculosis. Each time after he was ministered to in prayer, they would take an X-ray. We could see the progress of the healing. Each picture showed less and less of the disease until there was no more evidence of it. He was completely well.

We always prayed for a person until we were satisfied that the healing was complete. There was no dependence on the arm of man (flesh).

Mr. W. A. Fay suffered from cancer of the stomach. He has been ministered to perhaps thirty times.

For the first ten days there was no evidence of healing whatever or a subsiding of his suffering. After that, there was a gradual subsiding; then color began to return to his face, and he began to put on flesh.

Now he can eat anything and everything, and as much of it as he can get! And that is not all, beloved. He found the Lord and Savior Jesus Christ while the process was going on, and he says that is the big part of it.

I guess the Lord knows how to open doors in people's hearts. A good many Christians overlook the fact that Jesus Christ made the ministry of healing just as broad as He could make it.

To the Seventy (Luke 10:8,9), He said, ". . . into whatsoever city ye enter, and they receive you . . . heal the sick that are therein." And then what did He tell them to do? ". . . Say unto them, The kingdom of God is come nigh unto you."

I once lived near a man who was sick unto death. Some went to him and told him he had to be baptized, or he would die and go to hell.

I have always said that was a form of coercion, and Jesus Christ never used it. He was too much of a gentleman. He never took advantage of a man when he was down to grind his soul and try to influence him to be a Christian.

If the man was sick, Jesus went and healed him by the power of God. Then, when that man was healed, the natural response of his loving soul led him to Christ.

I wonder, have you ever paid attention to the different occasions in reading the Scriptures when the Voice of God is mentioned?

You know, the thing that makes the Bible the Bible is the fact that somebody had an interview with God! Somebody heard from Heaven before there was any Bible. Then the conversation or the incident was recorded, and these became the Word of God.

Now, the Word of God is indestructible, because it was a real Voice, a real experience. God really did or said something, and the record of it is true.

It is very simple to prove the inspiration of the Bible. Every child is taught to "prove" whether or not his sum in mathematics is correct.

If you have doubts, questions, and fears concerning the Bible and its inspiration, we know that if one soul ever heard from Heaven, another soul may.

If one soul ever had an interview with God, another soul may.

If any man ever knew his sins were forgiven at any period, another man may know his sins are forgiven now.

If a man or woman ever were healed by the power of God, then men and women can be healed again.

The only thing necessary is to return again in soul experience to that same place of intimacy where the first individual met God.

That is the way you prove the Word of God.

That is the reason Christians love the Word of God.

That is the reason the Word of God becomes the thing men live by, the thing men will die for. The Word of God becomes a present, living reality to them — not just a theory.

— February 1, 1922
Thatcher, Oregon

In my church in South Africa we published a paper in 10,000 lots. We would have the printers send them to the church, and we would lay them out on the front platform in packages of 100 and 200. At the evening service I would call certain people from the congregation (that I knew to be in contact with the living God) to come and kneel around the packages and lay their hands on them.

We asked God to not only bless the reading matter in the paper that the message of Christ should come through the words printed on the paper, but that the paper itself become filled with the Spirit of God, just as the handkerchiefs became filled with the power of God. (Acts 19:12.)

I could show you thousands of letters from people in all parts of the world, telling me that the Spirit of God came upon them when they received our paper. Not only were they healed, but the joy of God came into their hearts and many were saved.

One woman wrote from South America: "I received your paper. When I took it into my hands, my body began to vibrate so, I could hardly sit on the chair. I did not understand it. I laid the paper down, and after a while took it up again. As soon as I had it in my hands, I shook again. The third time I picked up the paper, the Spirit of God came upon me so powerfully, I was baptized in the Holy Ghost."

Beloved, do you see that this message and this quality of the Spirit contains the thing that confuses all the philosophers and all the practice of philosophy in the world? It shows the clearest distinction which characterizes the real religion of Jesus Christ. It is distinct from all other religions and all other ministries.

The ministry of Christianity is the ministry of the Spirit. It is the Spirit of God that inhabits the words, that speaks to the spirit of another and reveals Christ in and through him.

Miss K. is a woman I term a victim of surgery — operated on 26 times, then left to die. She was an invalid for 13 years, and was visited and ministered to by different physicians for 6 years.

(I know you will pardon me if I speak with great plainness. I must in order to let you know what God has done in this woman's life.)

In one operation, an incision was made connecting the rectum and the vagina. That wound refused to heal. Three times the wound was sewn up, but to no avail. Also, she was thought to be tubercular, and no doubt she was.

One day this dear soul called Brother Westwood to minister to her. We commenced to pray the prayer of faith on her behalf, and right away the wounds on her body began to heal until all the outer wounds were healed. If you were close enough to her, you could see scars all down her throat and neck where some of these 26 operations had been performed.

Now I want you to see the power of God. When she discovered that the rectal incision had not healed, it became a matter of special prayer. Soon her bowels ceased to operate, she had no movement for 28 days. Think of it! If such a thing occurs in your life for three or four days, you think you are going to die.

Note the purpose of God: During those 28 days when there was no movement whatever, the wound healed up.

Miss K. went to the south side of town to do some dressmaking; but while working, she became unconscious due to the gas pressing upon her heart and lungs.

A physician was called. In his examination, he discovered that the incision was perfectly healed, but during the long time that the lower end of the rectum had not been used it had adhesed. Now according to the doctor, she could never have a movement of the bowels until she was operated on.

They were about to carry Miss K. off to the hospital when she became conscious and said, "No more operations for me, even if I die. I have committed my body, my soul, and my spirit to God!"

So they took her home.

She came down to the Tabernacle to drill the children for their Christmas entertainment. On her way home, she fainted on the street and was carried to the emergency hospital. They examined her there and corroborated the statement of the other physician.

They were in the act of taking her to St. Luke's when she became conscious and said, "No, sir! No more operations for me, even if I die."

When they asked her what she wanted to do, she told them she was coming to my home. That was on Saturday, November 27th.

On Sunday afternoon, November 28th, she was sitting in the audience. As prayer was being offered, she said it seemed as though a hand was laid upon her body (abdomen) and another hand on her head. Then a Voice said "You are healed."

She left the Audience Room and became perfectly normal, and has remained a normal woman ever since.

Beloved, people who oppose this ministry and do not understand it will say, "That is all right. We know God does do such things as that on special occasions, but they are special cases. Paul had a thorn in the flesh. He prayed three times that it might be healed, and the Lord said, 'Paul, My grace is sufficient for you' (2 Cor. 12:9), and he was not healed."

Who said so? Who gave you the interpretation? Did you hear the Voice of God, or are you repeating the old fable that has come down through theology for 100 years?

Do you not see, beloved, just one of the many tricks the old theological dodgers use to get away from the responsibility of praying the prayer of faith that saves the sick?

My, the Church has had a time trying to dodge this issue of healing! They come up with Paul's thorn in the flesh.

Paul said, "I wrote this large letter with my own hand" (Gal. 6:11), and they interpret that to read that he had bad eyes. Who said so?

On another occasion, the people said they loved Paul so much they would pluck out their eyes for him. I believe they would have cut off their leg or their right arm, too, if it would have done him any good, but none of these things argue for a moment that there was anything wrong with his leg, his arm, or his eyes.

Paul prayed three times. The first two times he was not conscious of the answer. He prayed again, bless God, and this time God met his faith and said to him, "Paul, My grace is sufficient for you."

Apply it, Paul. Dive in, Paul, and take all you want of the grace of God. It will fix your thorn in the flesh and everything else that is troubling you.

— January 23, 1916
Spokane, Washington

We went to Lourdes, France, in the company of a group of Church of England people who had been appointed as a committee to visit all the institutions of repute along the healing lines in Europe.

We visited a Catholic institution where healing is obtained by the waters of Lourdes. They maintain a board of 200 physicians whose business it is to examine all candidates and report on them.

We also visited the greatest hypnotic institution for healing in the world while at Lourdes. This institution sent its representatives to demonstrate their method before the Catholic board of 200 physicians. Hearing of our committee, they invited us to come before this body and demonstrate healing along our lines.

I agreed to take part, if I were given the final demonstration. The committee selected five candidates — people who had been pronounced absolutely incurable.

The hypnotists tried their several methods without success.

I then had the five candidates placed in chairs in a row upon the platform, in view of this large audience of physicians and scientists. I then prayed over each of them separately and at the same time laid my hands upon them.

Three were instantly healed, a fourth recovered in a few days, and one died.

— 1909

In 1901, I joined the Dowie Institution and moved to Zion City, Illinois, with the objective of becoming a student and teacher of divine healing. I was made manager of Dowie's Building Department. During that year we handled business amounting to $1.2 million, or $100,000 per month. We issued 1,200 building contracts.

This was the year John Alexander Dowie made his trip from Zion City to New York City, taking 3,000 people with him in ten trains. We had a road choir of 1,200 selected voices and a road processional of 100 church officers.

Dowie rented Madison Square Garden, which holds 20,000 people. The New York City Police said some nights they turned away as many as 100,000 people. The streets were congested for four blocks away.

In 1904, when Dowie's financial affairs were entangled, I left Zion City practically broke, my holdings in the Dowie property having become depreciated at his death.

One Saturday night in South Africa, the church was packed. All available standing room was occupied as men stood shoulder to shoulder. The majority of them were men from the Tattersall Racing Club. Most were Jews. They included horsemen of all classes: bookies, jockeys, stablemen, racetrack gamblers, etc.

I was preaching on the power of God and, in a strong spirit, was endeavoring to demonstrate that Jesus Christ is the same yesterday, today, and forever; that His power is as great as it ever was; and that the only qualification for touching God for anything is faith in Him. The audience was greatly moved.

At this point, I observed a gentleman and two ladies trying to squeeze through the people who were standing in the aisles. I asked the crowd to separate, if possible, to permit the ladies to come through, and I tried to arrange seating space for them on the steps of the platform.

As they approached, I observed that one of the ladies held her arms perfectly stiff. She did not move them at all. By instinct, I knew at once that she was a rheumatic cripple.

When she got to the platform, I asked, "What is the reason you do not move your arms?"

She said, "My shoulders are set from rheumatics."

I said, "How long have they been like this?"

She replied, "Ten years."

I inquired if she had been treated by physicians.

She replied, "I have been discharged from three hospitals as incurable."

"What hospitals?"

She answered, "Kimberley, Johannesburg, and Pretoria."

Then addressing the gentleman who accompanied her, I asked, "Do you know this lady?"

He said, "Yes, she is my sister-in-law."

I said, "Do you know her story to be correct?"

"Absolutely," he said.

I asked her what she had come for.

She replied, "In the hope that me Lord would heal me."

I inquired, "Do you wish me to pray for you for healing?"

"Yes," she said.

Addressing the noisy crowd in the aisles and around the doors, I said, "You men never saw Jesus heal a person in your life. You do not know anything about this matter. You have never witnessed an exhibition of the power of God, and therefore you should be considerate enough to keep still, confess your ignorance of such matters, and learn.

"This is what I want: Select two men from your group, and let then come and see for themselves if this woman's arms are stiff, as she states."

I waited for them to make their selection. Finally, they put forward two men. One was a barber, a very intelligent gentleman. I learned afterwards he was an American.

They examined the lady's arms critically and found them to be as she had said — quite immovable.

I asked the men, "Have you finished your examination? Are you satisfied her condition is as stated?"

They said, "We are."

"Then stand back, for I am going to pray that the Lord will heal this woman."

Placing my hands on her shoulders, I commanded in the name of Jesus Christ, the Son of God, that this rheumatic devil that bound the woman be cast out. In Christ's name I commanded it to go, rebuking it with all the energy of my soul.

The power of God flashed through me like a burning fire until perspiration burst from the woman's face.

Then, taking her by the hands, I said, "In the name of Jesus Christ, put your arms up!"

The right arm went up.

Then I said, "In the name of Jesus Christ put the other arm up, too."

She instantly obeyed. Her arms had become free!

As I moved her arms, making the shoulders rotate, I heard a grinding sound in the joints. I said to the two men from the audience, "You have never heard a dry joint in your life. Come put your ear to this woman's back while I make her arms move." As they did, I moved her arms, and the shoulder joints ground, because the oil had not yet returned to them.

In the woman's delight at being healed, she threw up her hands, praised God, and started for the door. The crowd parted for her, and she disappeared. I did not see her again for some months.

My Consecration as a Christian

I, this day, consecrate my entire life to glorify my Heavenly Father by my obedience to the principles of Jesus Christ through the power of the Holy Spirit. All my effort from now on will be directed in an effort to demonstrate the righteousness of God in whatsoever I may be engaged.

Principle 1

All the things earthly that I possess shall not be considered my own, but belonging to my Heavenly Father, and shall be held in trust by me to be used and directed by the wisdom of the Spirit of God, as the law of love of men as Christ loved them may dictate.

If at any time God should raise up men wiser than myself, I will gladly commit my all to their use and turn over all my possessions to them for distribution.

If at any time in my life I should be engaged in any earthly business and should employ men to aid me in conducting it, I shall reward them justly and equally, comparing their own energy expended with my own after adding a sufficient amount to my own to cover all risk that may be involved in the operation of my business.

I shall consider my employees my equals with rights to the blessings of nature and life equal to my own. I shall not strive to elevate myself to a position of comfort above the rest of my employees and shall direct all my efforts to bring all mankind to an equal plane, where all enjoy the comforts of life and fellowship together.

Principle 2

I shall not cease to cry to God and implore Him to deliver mankind from the effects of sin so long as sin lasts, but shall cooperate with God in the redemption of mankind.

I will have seasons of prayer and fasting in behalf of mankind, weeping and bewailing their lost condition and imploring God to grant them repentance unto life as the Spirit of God may lead me.

Principle 3

I shall live my life in meekness, never defending my own personal rights, but shall leave all judgment to God Who judges righteously and rewards all according to their works.

I shall not render evil for evil or railing for railing, but shall bless all and do good to enemies in return for evil.

By God's grace I shall keep all hardness and harshness out of my life and actions, but shall be gentle and unassuming, not professing above what God has imparted to me, nor lifting myself above my brethren.

Principle 4

I shall consider righteous acts as more necessary to life and happiness than food and drink, and not let myself be bribed or coerced into any unrighteous action for any earthly consideration.

Principle 5

By God's grace I will always be merciful, forgiving those who have transgressed against me and endeavoring to correct the ills of humanity instead of merely punishing them for their sins.

Principle 6

I shall not harbor any impure thoughts in my mind, but shall endeavor to make my every act uplifting.

I shall regard my procreative organs sacred and holy and never use them for any purpose other than that which God created them for.

I shall regard the home as sacred and always guard my actions in the presence of the opposite sex, so as not to cause a man and his wife to break their vows to one another. I shall be chaste with the opposite sex who are married, considering them as sisters. I shall be careful not to cause them undue pain by playing on their affections.

Principle 7

I will always strive to be a peacemaker. First, by being peaceful myself and avoiding all unfruitful contentions, and treating all with justice and regarding their rights and their free agency, never trying to force any to my point of view.

If I should offend anyone knowingly, I shall immediately apologize.

I will not scatter evil reports about any person and so try to defame their character, or repeat things that I am not certain of being true.

I will strive to remove the curse of strife among brethren by acting as a peacemaker.

Principle 8

I shall not become discouraged when I am persecuted on account of the righteousness mentioned above nor murmur on account of any suffering I undergo, but shall gladly give my life rather than depart from this high standard of life, rejoicing because I know I have a great reward in Heaven.

I shall strive to make the above principles the ideal of all the world and give my life and energy to see mankind get the power from God to practice the same.

— John G. Lake

Significant Events in the Life of John G. Lake

March 18, 1870	Born at St. Mary's, Ontario, Canada.
1886	Moved with parents to United States and settled in Sault Ste. Marie, Michigan.
October 1891	Admitted into Methodist ministry in Chicago. Declined pastorate to found two newspapers.
February 1893	Married Miss Jennie Stevens of Newberry, Michigan.
April 28, 1898	Wife instantly healed under the ministry of John Alexander Dowie, founder of Zion, Illinois.
1901	Moved to Zion City.
1904	Left Zion City. Moved to Chicago and bought a seat on Chicago Board of Trade.
April 1907	Having received the baptism in the Holy Spirit, Lake abandoned his successful insurance business, disposed of his wealth, and embarked on an independent evangelistic work, living by faith.
April 19, 1908	Left Indianapolis for historic five-year missionary journey to Africa.

May 1908	Arrived in South Africa.
1909	Returned to United States for six months to hold evangelistic services and raised funds to take eight missionaries back to South Africa.
January 1910	Lake and his missionary party returned to South Africa.
1910	Founded Apostolic Church and was elected its president; 125 white and 500 native congregations eventually organized.
1912	Returned from expedition to Kalahari Desert to find that his wife had died unexpectedly of a stroke and had been buried. With his seven children, Lake went home to the United States and never returned to Africa.
November 27, 1913	Married Miss Florence Switzer of Milwaukee and fathered five children.
1914	Founded the Apostolic Church in Spokane, where the famous Healing Rooms attracted thousands from the United States and other countries. Branch churches were founded in subsequent years in Portland, San Diego, and other cities.
September 16, 1935	Went to be with the Lord at age 65 while still pastoring Spokane.

Photographs

Postcard photo taken at Azusa Street Mission in Los Angeles, California.

Front row left to right: "Daddy" Seymour and John G. Lake.

Second row left to right: Mr. Adams, F.F. Bosworth, and Brother Tom.

x pect to go to St Louis
3 weeks.

John G. Lake Healing Rooms Staff at Spokane, Washington.

These men and women of God saw 100,000 confirmed healings in five years.

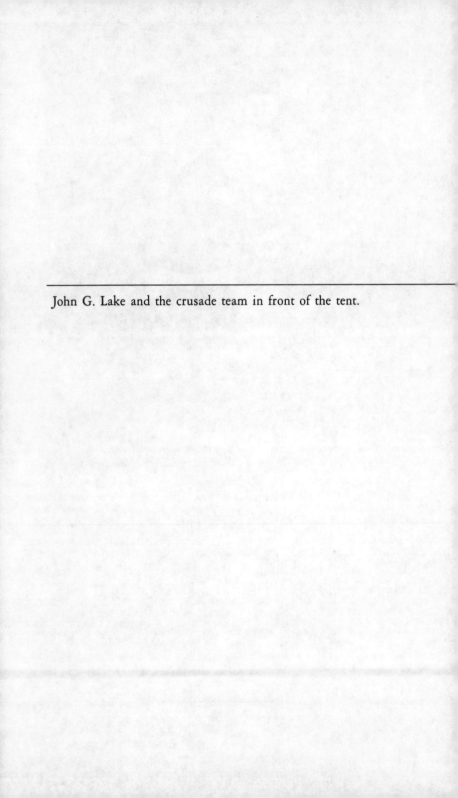

John G. Lake and the crusade team in front of the tent.

Other **Living Classic Books** from Harrison House

Kathryn Kuhlman — Roberts Liardon

A Diary of Signs and Wonders — Maria Woodworth-Etter

Questions and Answers on Spiritual Gifts — Howard Carter

Healing the Sick — T. L. Osborn

Smith Wigglesworth: A Man Who Walked With God
— George Stormont

Smith Wigglesworth Remembered — W. Hacking

Smith Wigglesworth: The Secret of His Power

— Albert Hibbert

Cry of the Spirit — Roberts Liardon
(previously unpublished works of Smith Wigglesworth)

John G. Lake: A Man Without Compromise — Wilford Reidt

Azusa Street Till Now — Clara Davis

Available from your local bookstore,
or by writing:

Harrison House
P. O. Box 35035
Tulsa, OK 74153

For additional copies
of this book
in Canada contact:

Word Alive
P. O. Box 670
Niverville, Manitoba
CANADA R0A 1EO

The Harrison House Vision

Proclaiming the truth and the power
Of the Gospel of Jesus Christ
With excellence;

Challenging Christians to
Live victoriously,
Grow spiritually,
Know God intimately.